TONI MORRISON

TONI MORRISON

Great American Writer
by Lisa R. Rhodes

A Book Report Biography
FRANKLIN WATTS
A Division of Grolier Publishing
New York / London / Hong Kong / Sydney
Danbury, Connecticut

Excerpt from Toni Morrison's 1993 Nobel Prize Lecture reprinted with
permission of The Nobel Foundation in Stockholm, Sweden.

Cover illustration by Dave Klaboe, interpreted from a photograph ©
Retna Ltd./Falour/Stills

Photographs ©: AP/Wide World Photos: 72; Archive Photos: 19 (American
Stock), 13 (Reuters/Pressen Bild); Black River Historical Society, Lorain,
OH: 21, 25, 28; Corbis Sygma: 77 (Danny Hoffman); Corbis-Bettmann:
107 (Michel Bourquard), 105 (Mitch Gerber), 40, 51 (UPI), 71, 75;
Courtesy of Howard University Archives: 33, 36; Everett Collection, Inc.:
56 (CSU Archives), 15, 88, 90; Liaison Agency, Inc.: 2 (Ulf Anderson);
Photofest: 31, 48; Retna Ltd./Camera Press Ltd.: 93 (Jim Cooper), 101
(Walter McBride), 110 (Susan Stava); Texas Southern University,
Heartman Collection: 38; The Daily Princetonian: 11, 84;
The Morning Journal, Lorain, OH: 98.

Visit Franklin Watts on the Internet at:
http://publishing.grolier.com

Library of Congress Cataloging-in-Publication Data

Rhodes, Lisa Renee.
    Toni Morrison : great American writer / by Lisa R. Rhodes.
      p. cm.—(A book report biography)
    Includes bibliographical references and index.
    ISBN 0-531-11677-8 (lib. bdg.) 0-531-15555-2 (pbk.)
    1. Morrison, Toni—Juvenile literature. 2. Novelists, American—20th
century—Biography—Juvenile literature. 3. Afro–American women novelists—Biography—Juvenile literature. [1. Morrison, Toni. 2. Authors, American. 3. Women—Biography. 4. Afro-Americans—Biography.] I. Title. II.
Series.

    PS3563.O8749 Z829 2001
    813'.54—dc21
    [B]   00-032077

CONTENTS

CHAPTER ONE

AFRICAN-AMERICAN, FEMALE, AND FIRST

Toni Morrison walked down the stairs at the Concert Hall in Stockholm, Sweden, carefully like a queen. Her gray dreadlocks swept the nape of her neck in long tendrils. Her long flowing black gown, made by designer Bill Blass, almost touched the floor, and her black and bright-pink shoulder wrap cradled her golden-brown shoulders. Her escort, King Carl XVI Gustaf of Sweden, gently held her arm as they descended the stairs. Morrison was now a member of the world's literary royalty. She had come to Stockholm in December 1993 to receive the Nobel Prize in Literature. She was the first African-American woman to receive the award.

"This is a palpable tremor of delight for me. It was wholly unexpected and so satisfying," Morrison told a *New York Times* reporter in October 1993 when the announcement of her win was made. "Regardless of what we say and truly believe about the irrelevance of prizes and their relationship to the real work, nevertheless, this is a signal honor for me."[1]

Morrison, then 62, received the Nobel Prize for an exceptional career as a writer. She had written six novels, all telling the triumphs and tragedies of African-Americans in the 1800s and 1900s. Her books—*The Bluest Eye* (1970), *Sula* (1973), *Song of Solomon* (1977), *Tar Baby* (1981), *Beloved* (1987), and *Jazz* (1992)—had captured the attention of critics and readers throughout the United States and the world. Her works have been translated into more than twenty different languages. The Nobel Committee of the Swedish Academy, which awards the prize, praised Morrison for her literary efforts in its announcement. The academy called Morrison "a literary artist of finest work," who "gives life to an essential aspect of American reality." Said the Academy, "She delves into the language itself, a language she wants to liberate from the fetters of race. And she addresses us with the luster of poetry."[2]

For almost twenty years, Morrison has created memorable African-American characters who struggle to live their lives as full individuals and members of the African-American community. Her characters must often overcome the brutality of slavery, racial and economic oppression, and sexism, but they rely on their own inner strengths, the bonds of the African-American community, spirituality, and their love of African-American culture, to shape their lives. "It's true [my characters] go through difficult circumstances," Morrison once told an interviewer. But by the end of her novels, "people always know something profound and wonderful."[3]

Her works had helped to change the face of American literature—a literature that once told only the conquests of white men with white women as minor characters. Morrison's work introduced lyrical prose, storytelling, African-American folklore, and African-American history to the American literary establishment. African-American literature, also dominated by male characters, was similarly changed when Morrison introduced the female point of view and female sensitivities—and made them credible. "She has taken the specific and often terrible history of African-American people in America and lofted it into the tireless realm of myth," wrote critic Michiko Kakutani in *The New York Times*.[4]

Morrison, who won the Pulitzer Prize for Fiction a few years earlier, had not expected to win the Nobel. Morrison woke up to write at about 4:30 A.M. one crisp October morning in 1993. The phone rang a few hours later. "I knew it was terrible news," Morrison told *The New York Times*.

Instead, the news was joyous—a friend had called to tell Morrison that she had won the Nobel. "It took a long time for me to accept it," Morrison admitted. Several hours later, the secretary of the Swedish Academy called Morrison to deliver the good news and to let her know that a confirmation letter was on its way to her home. "I said 'Why don't you send me a fax,'" Morrison said jokingly. "Somehow, I felt that if I saw a fax, I'd know it wasn't a dream or somebody's hallucination," she told *The New York Times*. "I'll tell you one thing, we're going to have a big party here tonight!"[5]

The Nobel Prizes, founded by Alfred Bernhard Nobel, a Swedish scientist, have been given each year since 1901. The prizes are given in six different fields of study to a person who has made a valuable contribution to the "good of humanity." The prizes are awarded in physics, chemistry, medicine, international peace, economics, and literature.

The Nobel Prize in Literature is given to the person who has created the "most distinguished work of an idealistic nature." The award is usually given for a lifetime of literary efforts, rather than a single book. Prizewinners receive the award on December 10, the anniversary of Alfred Nobel's death.

Morrison answered many phone calls on the morning she heard the news. By 10:00 A.M., she had turned off the telephone to take a hot bath. She also refused her publisher's invitation to hold a press conference about the announcement. Morrison decided to go to work instead. A professor of creative writing and humanities at Princeton University in New Jersey, Morrison met a crowd of news reporters at the university who wanted to know her response to the honor. Morrison continued to teach her classes for the day, undistracted by the media attention.

Morrison talks with reporters on the day she learned about her Nobel Prize.

Morrison had to prepare for a full week of celebratory activities. The Nobel Prize Committee had set up a dinner, a concert, and press conferences for Morrison. Many literary dignitaries would come to see her receive the award at the Swedish Academy and hear her Nobel Prize lecture. But soon after the Nobel announcement, Morrison found she hardly had any time to write her lecture—instead she had to decide what to wear for the award ceremony. "I called someone at the Nobel Committee," Morrison told *Time* magazine five years after receiving the award, "and I said 'Look, if you're going to keep giving prizes to women—and I hope you do—you're going to have to give us more warning. Men can rent tuxedos. I have to get shoes. And I have to get a dress.'"[6]

Despite her earlier concerns, when Morrison arrived in Stockholm in early December, she arrived in style. An audience of four hundred well-wishers at the Swedish Academy heard her Nobel Prize lecture about the importance of literature in shaping a humane society. Part of Morrison's lecture read:

"Oppressive language does more than represent violence; it is violence; it does more than represent limits of knowledge; it limits knowledge. Whether it is obscuring state language or the faux-language of the mindless media; whether it is the proud but calcified language of the academy, or the commodity-driven language of science; whether it is the malign language of law—without ethics, or language designed for the estrangement of minorities, hiding its racist plunder in its literary cheek—it must be rejected, altered, and exposed."[7]

Morrison received a standing ovation for her lecture. No one doubted that she deserved the Nobel Prize and she was presented with the

Toni Morrison receives the Nobel Prize from King Carl Gustav of Sweden.

award at a lavish ceremony. In 1993, the winner of the Nobel Prize in Literature received a monetary award of $825,000.

When Morrison returned to the United States, however, some of her fellow writers questioned whether she deserved the award. Charles Johnson, author of the novel *Middle Passage*, was critical, insisting that Morrison won the award because she "has been the beneficiary of goodwill." Johnson, in a *Washington Post* article, said Morrison, who began writing in the early 1970s (the years after the Civil Rights Movement and the beginning of the Women's Movement), had managed to combine the calls for African-American pride and equity among African-American women. "But when that particular brand of politics is filtered through her [poetic] writing, the result is often offensive, harsh," Johnson noted. "Whites are portrayed badly. Men are. African-American men are." In his final comments, Johnson said Morrison's award was "a triumph of political correctness."[8]

Other writers came to Morrison's defense. "No one writes more beautifully than Toni Morrison," said Alice Walker, author of *The Color Purple*. "She has consistently explored issues of true complexity and terror and love in the lives of blacks. Harsh criticism has not dissuaded her. Prizes have not trapped her. She is a writer who deserves this honor."[9]

Morrison had not been a stranger to controversy in her career. In the late 1980s, she had
been in the midst of another dispute. During this
time, other writers wondered why Morrison had
not received another important award, and they
wrote to *The New York Times Book Review* to
complain. Some literary critics have complained

Author Alice Walker

her writing style is overdone. Some readers have complained her novels are hard to understand. Political conservatives have also criticized her scholarly exploration of the role of race in American literature. Through it all, Morrison has persevered and never lost sight of her first love—writing.

According to literature scholar Trudier Harris, Morrison is a literary giant who is as important to American culture as one of our finest athletes. "By any standard of literary evaluation, Toni Morrison is a phenomenon in the classic sense of a once-in-a-lifetime rarity, the literary equivalent of Paul Robeson, Michael Jordan . . .," Harris wrote in *World Literature Today*. Morrison has "a place in the canons of world literature."[10]

Morrison would withstand controversy to become a master writer, editor, teacher, and mentor to upcoming African-American writers who also aspire to share their vision of the world. "There were plenty of roadblocks along the way," Morrison told *Time* magazine when recalling her writing career. "The world back then didn't expect much from a little black girl, but my father and mother certainly did. She [Morrison's mother] was still alive when I won the Nobel,

> **"There were plenty of roadblocks along the way,"**

although she died three months later. She was delighted, but not surprised."[11]

Toni Morrison's life has been one of great expectations. It all began in a small Midwestern steel-mill town in a family headed by proud and strong parents who shaped Morrison's view of life—and her writing.

CHAPTER TWO

AT HOME WITH FATHER

Ardelia and John Solomon Willis woke every morning before sunrise to work the crop fields on 88 acres (36 hectares) of farmland Willis owned in Greenville, Alabama in the early 1900s. They worked the land together and raised their children there. Southern land was a link to the Willis family's past.

Willis and his parents were once slaves—among the millions of blacks whose ancestors were taken from Africa on slave ships and held in bondage for life by white Americans in the northern and southern United States. The North eventually outlawed slavery, but the South continued the practice. The slaves were made to plant and harvest cotton and other crops that their owners would later sell. The slaves never shared in the money, land, or other resources that came from their life's work. Instead, the ancestors of the

Many slaves worked the land, including Morrison's ancestors in her grandfather's family.

Willis family and other blacks endured whippings, physical torture, degradation, and the pain of being sold away from each other—separating husband from wife and mother from child.

In 1863, President Abraham Lincoln signed the Emancipation Proclamation, granting legal freedom to African-Americans in slavery, including John Solomon Willis, who was born a slave.

His granddaughter, Chloe Anthony Wofford, known later as Toni Morrison, would become one of America's most highly respected writers. She would earn that honor, in part for retelling the stories of African-American slaves and their families. "Fathers and sons, mothers and daughters—these bonds are essential to Ms. Morrison, who plays out the drama of slavery and racism in the most intimate human relationships," wrote a journalist in the *Wall Street Journal* in 1993, some sixty years after Chloe's birth.[1]

Chloe Anthony Wofford was born on February 18, 1931, in Lorain, Ohio. Her mother, Ramah Willis, had moved to Ohio with her parents from Alabama in 1912, after the family lost their land to a group of white southerners in a shady business agreement. Ramah later married George Wofford, a proud African-American laborer from Georgia. The Wofford family settled in Lorain and Chloe was born two years after the birth of their first daughter. The Woffords later had two sons.

Hard work was not a stranger to either the Wofford or Willis families. George Wofford held three jobs at the same time to provide shelter and food for his family, although work was extremely difficult to find in the early 1930s. Chloe was born during the Great Depression—a time when the U.S. economy almost collapsed. Many banks

The house where Chloe was born

failed, many people lost their homes, and count-
less numbers of people stood in line at soup
kitchens to get food. Wofford worked in a car
wash, at a road-construction site, in steel mills,
and at a shipyard to earn money. Wofford was
never ashamed of the type of work he did—
instead he was motivated to do his best. He
worked diligently in the shipyard to weld perfect

seams on the sides of steel ships. He often wrote his name after each seam as proof of his success. Grandfather John Solomon Willis worked as a carpenter and a coal miner soon after his family moved to the North.

Ramah Wofford also held her head high. At one time, the Woffords, like many Depression-era families, relied on the federal government for assistance to make ends meet. The Woffords signed up for the government's food-relief program and once found bugs in the flour and other food items they received from the government. Ramah was insulted, but she did not bow her head. She quickly wrote a letter of protest to President Franklin Delano Roosevelt to air her concerns about the quality of the food in the relief program.

Ramah also showed her inner strength when her husband was unemployed. The Woffords could not pay the $4 rent, and one day found an "Evicted" sign pasted on their front door by the landlord. Ramah quickly removed the sign and ripped it up. The landlord did not give up, though. Sometime later, the landlord burnt the Wofford home down in retaliation for the unpaid rent.

"It was this hysterical, out-of-the-ordinary, bizarre form of evil," Chloe would recall years later in an interview with a journalist. "If you internalized it [the tragedy], you'd be truly and thoroughly depressed because that's how much your life meant. For four dollars a month, somebody would just burn you to a crisp."[2]

Luckily, no one was hurt in the fire, although Chloe, her mother, and sister were at home when it started. Despite the many hardships the family faced, Chloe and her siblings never saw their parents break under the strain, and they passed their formidable strength and self-esteem on to their children. "Social obstacles, economic obstacles, or racism were obstacles, but we ourselves were extraordinary and superior people," Chloe said years later. "My parents also responded to life like that."[3]

Life for African-Americans was far from easy—particularly during the Great Depression. African-Americans in the South struggled with the decreasing number of agricultural jobs, while most African-Americans—like the Woffords and Willis families—had moved to the North hoping to find employment, housing, and a better life. Southern blacks had to live with legal racial segregation—laws that prevented them from eating in public restaurants with whites, using the same public bathrooms, or even attending the same public schools. African-Americans were also restricted from voting. In addition, white supremacy groups, such as the Ku Klux Klan, terrorized blacks. The Klan was known for harassing and even lynching African-Americans who dared to try to improve their lives by trying to vote or owning a plot of land. While segregation laws were not as prevalent in the North, African-Americans still faced discrimination in housing, employment, and the use of public facilities. For example, Chloe, her siblings, and other blacks in Lorain, were not allowed to swim in Lake Erie during the summer, while whites enjoyed the lake whenever they wanted to.

However, relations between blacks and whites in Lorain were better than in some parts of America, North or South. Chloe grew up in a fully integrated community. Her neighbors were Irish, Italian, Greek, and German. The one common factor between blacks and whites in town was their economic class. Most of the families were blue-collar, working-class people, and this circumstance seemed to bond everyone together. "We were all in one economic class and therefore mutually dependent upon one another," Chloe explained years later. "There was a great deal of sharing of food and services, and caring. If someone was ill, people might come and take care of him or her, regardless of race."[4]

Chloe and her siblings also went to school with white children. "They were my friends . . . There was no awe, or fear," Chloe told a journalist years later, noting that only when she became a teenager did she notice "how clear the lines really were." Said Chloe, "But when I was in first grade, nobody thought I was inferior. I was the only black in class and the only child who could read!"[5]

> **"I was the only black in class and the only child who could read!"**

George Wofford felt quite differently about relations between blacks and whites. George was convinced that some whites could not be trusted and that the black man had to be careful not to be taken for granted.

Chloe (second from left, first row) participated in many school activities, including the Library Aids.

George's life in Georgia shaped his perspective of white Americans. The constant threat of physical violence and the legal barriers to social progress were proof to him that the scales of justice were tipped generously toward whites—not blacks. The only advantage given to African-Americans was their humanity. "My father [in that sense] really felt that black people were better than all white people because their position was [inherently] a moral one," Chloe said.[6]

As a matter of fact, George felt so strongly about white Americans that he would not allow whites into the Wofford home. Chloe recalled years later in a 1998 interview with "60 Minutes," the television news program, that white insurance salesmen could enter the home only when her father was not there.[7]

Ramah was more likely to believe that with education, people could overcome their racial prejudices. While her husband taught the children about the separation of blacks and whites, Ramah's devotion to the Christian church shaped a more spiritual perspective—one that favored conscientious protest. Ramah dared to sit in the white-only section of the local movie theater to see Saturday matinees, rather than sit in the section reserved for blacks. For Ramah, integrating a movie theater or writing a letter to the president were simply forms of protest.

George and Ramah worked together to instill a sense of racial pride in their children. Racism and racial discrimination were unfortunate realities of life for African-Americans, and the Woffords knew their children needed a solid cultural foundation to succeed in life. Chloe's parents and grandparents often shared stories taken in part from Africa about ghosts, supernatural events, folktales, and myths. These stories were handed down in both families after slavery, a custom in many African-American families. Children like Chloe and her siblings learn at an early age that the spirit world is a natural part of life—not something to fear or criticize. The Wofford children also gathered around the family's kitchen table to hear stories and listen to music. Ramah sang in church and often sang the gospel and work songs that the slaves sang among themselves as they worked in the fields. Grandfather Willis played the violin at family gatherings and often managed to earn a few dollars using his skills as a musician.

Chloe loved the family's music and stories. Years later, as an adult, she would recall how her adult relatives always asked the Wofford children about their dreams. These family influences helped to make Chloe an advanced student. By the time she graduated from Lorain High School—with honors—Chloe had studied Latin and had read most of Europe's classical literature,

Chloe as a high school senior

ranging from Russian authors such as Dostoyevsky and Tolstoy—authors of *Crime and Punishment* and *War and Peace*, respectively—and even Gustave Flaubert, the French author of *Madame Bovary*. She also enjoyed the writings of England's Jane Austen, the author of *Pride and Prejudice*. The Wofford family's link to Africa helped Chloe to appreciate her own heritage and the fine cultural works of other ethnic groups. But for many years she yearned to read books about the deep psychological and spiritual complexities of African-American life—books by African-Americans.

Chloe hoped to read such works someday, but she had no ambitions to become a writer herself, although she did manage to scribble a few notes about her experiences. For the most part, she spent her teenage years studying hard and helping to earn money for the family. At thirteen, Chloe worked part-time after school cleaning a white family's house. It was one experience, in addition to being barred from Lake Erie, that taught Chloe the harsh inequities between African-Americans and whites. The white family she worked for was far from friendly, and Chloe hated the long hours of hard work. But George Wofford would not let his daughter walk away from an important lesson in self-respect. "Girl, you don't live there. You live here. So go do your work, get your money, and come on home."[8] Chloe followed her father's advice and never again doubted her ability to face racial adversity.

She also learned an unspoken rule about some white Americans and their view of African-Americans. Years later in an interview with "60 Minutes," Chloe explained that although she is not prejudiced against all white Americans, her life experiences have taught her that some whites could not be trusted—they would "betray" her. Chloe called her attitude toward some whites a "constant vigilance and awareness" to ensure her physical, emotional, and spiritual well-being.[9]

College was the natural choice for Chloe after her success in high school. She decided to apply to Howard University in Washington, D.C., one of the largest mainly African-American universities in America. When Chloe graduated from high school in 1949, she thought she would become a ballerina, following in the footsteps of the famous Maria Tallchief. Tallchief, the daughter of an Osage American Indian father and a Scots-Irish mother, began her career at the New York City Ballet in 1947. Tallchief was known for her personal discipline and grace, qualities Chloe hoped to emulate. It seemed the educational opportunities at a predominantly African-American university would help Chloe achieve her dreams. After eighteen years at home with her defiant father, Chloe left Ohio for the northeastern United States to begin her life as a young woman. Her experience at Howard University would teach her more about African-Americans than she ever imagined.

In high school, Chloe dreamed of being a ballerina like Maria Tallchief.

CHAPTER THREE

"TONI" MORRISON

Not long after Chloe arrived on the campus of Howard University in the fall of 1949, she made two decisions that would greatly influence her adult life. She changed her name from Chloe to "Toni" (a shortened version of her middle name Anthony), because some classmates could not pronounce her name properly, and she joined the Howard University Players, a campus theater group made up of students and faculty members.

The Howard University Players performed works by William Shakespeare and other revered European playwrights during the school year. The performances complemented Toni's English literature major and her minor in the classics. In the summer, the group performed for African-American audiences throughout the South. Toni's travels in the southern states made her more familiar with the life and struggles of her parents and

Toni in the Howard University Players' production of Shakespeare's Richard III

grandparents who fled legal segregation and discrimination with hopes of better opportunities in the North. Toni was able to see first-hand the poor living conditions of many rural African-Americans who had not been able to progress past generations of working as sharecroppers. They worked for menial wages and endured segregated public bathrooms and movie theaters. Although Toni—the actress—had no interest in writing about the injustices she saw in the South, she was touched by the images she saw and the African-American people who came to her theatrical performances. These memories of African-Americans made a lasting impression on the literature she wrote years later.

Unfortunately, Toni discovered that many of her African-American classmates at Howard were not particularly interested in the common life of southern African-Americans—or in the history and contributions of African-Americans. Many of the faculty and students at Howard at that time had little interest in authentic African-American culture, although the university was founded in 1867 to train African-American preachers to serve free African-Americans after the Civil War. Toni found that the history, culture, and literature of Europeans and white Americans were taught in the classroom, rather than the works of blacks. This was common practice at many colleges, both black and white, in the 1940s. African-American studies did not become a widely taught subject in most schools and colleges until the Civil Rights Movement twenty years later.

On campus, students were preoccupied with the social status and skin color of their peers. Students from middle-class and upper middle-class backgrounds with light or fair complexions were preferred to students who came from humbler family origins and had darker skin tones. For example, Toni knew a female student who was not popular with the men on campus because of her dark brown skin. Their attitudes changed when they learned that her parents were rich. The men suddenly took an interest in the young woman and many asked her out on dates. Toni disapproved of young men's actions since they were only interested in her friend because she had money.

Toni participated in some of the social activities on campus—she joined Alpha Kappa Alpha, one of the many African-American sororities on campus, but tried her best to avoid engaging in some of the elitist, snobby attitudes and behaviors of her fellow students. Toni wanted to hold on to her family's working-class and southern roots and learn more about her African-American heritage without alienating the new middle-class social order she surprisingly found at Howard. It was a strange journey, but Toni was not afraid to test

Toni in her college yearbook

her newfound independence. Instead, she focused on her schoolwork. She graduated in 1953 and applied for a master's degree program at Cornell University.

Toni enrolled at Cornell to pursue a degree in English. She continued to love classic literature and decided to write her thesis paper on the works of William Faulkner and Virginia Woolf and the two authors' preoccupation with the theme of suicide. Toni graduated in 1955.

After her graduate studies, Toni decided to teach English. She applied for a teaching position at Texas Southern University (TSU) in Houston, Texas, and she was hired to teach introductory English to college freshmen. Toni did not mind returning to the South to teach. TSU became a place where she would celebrate African-American culture and learn more about the contributions of African-Americans—for the first time in her academic experience. "[I] began to think about black culture as a subject, as an idea, as a discipline," Toni recalled years later. "Before it had only been on a very personal level—my family."[1] Toni taught at the university for 1½ years.

Toni was not the only African-American to make a conscious connection to her racial and cultural roots and feel a sense of pride. In 1954, lawyers for the National Association for the Advancement of Colored People (NAACP), the

Toni worked as an English Instructor at Texas Southern University.

country's oldest civil rights organization, won an important legal battle on behalf of African-Americans. Thurgood Marshall, an African-American lawyer and graduate of Howard University Law School, argued before the U.S. Supreme Court that the legal separation of blacks and whites in public schools was unconstitutional—and the Court agreed. In the *Brown vs. Board of Education of Topeka* case, the Supreme Court declared that segregated schools prevent blacks (and other children of color) from receiving an equal education. In addition, Chief Justice Earl Warren also stated for the Court that the legal separation of the races—racial segregation—went against the principles of the fourteenth amendment to the Constitution. This amendment guarantees all U.S. citizens the right to equal protection under the law, regardless of their race.

On the heels of the 1954 *Brown* decision, African-Americans in Montgomery, Alabama, were taking part in a grassroots movement for African-American civil rights that was beginning to take shape. In 1955, Rosa Parks, a black seamstress, refused to give up her seat on a bus to a white passenger, and started a yearlong bus boycott. African-Americans throughout the city pledged not to use the city buses until the city agreed to abolish the custom of seating passengers according to their race. The boycott was a major nonviolent protest against the city's public officials in the effort to strike down unfair segregation laws.

Rosa Parks's courage—she was arrested and fined for her refusal to give up her seat—led the Montgomery Improvement Association (MIA), a

Rosa Parks

local civil rights group, to take the city to court on Mrs. Parks's behalf. The lawsuit eventually led to a Supreme Court ruling declaring that state and city laws permitting racial segregation on city buses were unconstitutional. Dr. Martin Luther King Jr., a young African-American Baptist minister, led the MIA, and would someday become the most prominent leader of the Civil Rights Movement. In the meantime, the *Brown* decision and the successful Montgomery bus boycott were legal victories that gave many African-Americans hope that their children would grow up in a society that guaranteed equal rights to all.

Dr. King and other civil rights leaders favored racial integration, but Toni's childhood experiences and family influences led her to favor all-African-American institutions, particularly public schools. "I was not in favor of integration, but I couldn't officially say that, because I knew the terror and abuses of segregation," she said years later. "But integration also meant that we [blacks] would not have a fine black college or a fine black education. I didn't know why the assumption was that black children were going to learn better if they were in the company of white children."[2] Toni worried that the Supreme Court ruling to desegregate public schools would mean the end of black educational institutions. She supported increased funding to African-American schools to provide better textbooks and notebooks and more well-trained teachers.

Toni's commitment to African-American education brought her back to Howard University in 1957 to teach English. Now in her mid-twenties, she enjoyed her life as a single woman, but a year later she fell in love and married a young architect named Harold Morrison. Toni Morrison and her new husband, who was born in Jamaica, settled into their new home in Washington, D.C., and became parents three years later. Their first son, Harold Ford Morrison, was born in 1961.

Morrison was busy with her newborn son, her teaching, and her new marriage when she heard about a writers' group on Howard's campus. Morrison still was not serious about a writing career, but she wanted to broaden her circle of friends and thought being in the company of writers and poets would be a refreshing change from her daily routine. The group met once a month and the members shared their own works, reading and discussing their writing with their peers. At first, Morrison decided to share some of the scribblings she wrote in high school. But soon she ran out of material and found that she had to share more recent work. Morrison wasn't quite sure what to do, but one night she started to write a story about a young African-American girl she had met as a child. The girl had revealed one of her deepest secrets—she told Morrison that she had prayed to God for blue eyes for two years. Morrison knew that the girl's secret revealed a hidden desire—to have blue eyes like "pretty" white girls. But the girl's prayers were never answered. Devastated, the girl gave up her faith in God because she felt she was doomed to live her life as a black person.

One evening, Morrison shared her short story about the girl with the writers' group. Her peers were impressed with her work and wanted to hear more. Despite the group's enthusiasm, though, Morrison set the story aside. She thought nothing more of her story, except that it had done well in the writers' group.

Two years later, Morrison, pregnant with her second child, made another important decision. She resigned from her teaching position at Howard and spent the summer in Europe with her husband and young son. When Morrison returned to the United States, her marriage was over, and she had no job. Harold Morrison went back to Jamaica, and Toni returned to her family in Lorain, Ohio, to give birth to her son, Slade Kevin Morrison, in 1964.

It was one of the most difficult times in Morrison's life, and she later described it as "bleak." Despite her unhappiness, Morrison was determined to move forward. She knew her family would help her in any way they could, but she desperately wanted to avoid becoming a burden to her parents and siblings. At age thirty-four, Morrison had two sons and she wanted to get on with her life, find a job, and build a future. Said Morrison, "I wanted to find out who I was and whether I was tough enough."[3]

_____

"I wanted to find out who I was and whether I was tough enough."

_____

Years later, Morrison would only briefly recall the unhappy years of her marriage. In 1979, Morrison spoke about the troubled six-year marriage in an interview with *The New York Times Magazine.* "Women in Jamaica are very subservient in their marriages," Morrison explained. "They never challenge their husbands. I was a constant nuisance to mine. He didn't need me making judgments about him, which I did. A lot."[4]

A year later, in 1965, Morrison and her sons moved to Syracuse, New York. Ramah Wofford worried that her daughter's decision to move meant the possibility that she would have few friends. But Morrison was not afraid. "You take the village with you," she told her mother. "There is no need for the community if you have a sense of it inside."[5]

Morrison's work in the classroom prepared her for an editorial position in a textbook division at the Syracuse office of Random House, a publishing company based in New York City. Morrison became an associate editor and went to work editing textbooks about African-American history and culture for elementary and high schools.

Toni Morrison was now on her own. In the next few years, literary critics would find her to be one of the country's most promising African-American writers of fiction. But that praise did not come without loneliness and hard work.

CHAPTER FOUR

A WRITER'S PEN

Pecola Breedlove hates herself. When she looks into the mirror, she finds no beauty in her brown skin, dark eyes, and tightly curled hair. She prayed to God for two years to make her beautiful and give her blue eyes, like the 1930s child film star Shirley Temple. Pecola believes she must be ugly. Perhaps that was why she was raped by her drunken father, Cholly, and later became pregnant. Perhaps that was why the baby was born but did not survive. Pecola needs a miracle. Blue eyes will certainly change her world—make it tender, caring, and loving—a world away from the poverty she lives in and the rejection she faces from her mother Pauline. Pecola prayed hard and asked Soaphead Church, a so-called minister, to help her. But will her prayers be answered?

Toni Morrison created the character Pecola for her first novel, *The Bluest Eye*, during late-night writing sessions at her new home in Syracuse.

During the day, she worked at her publishing job, editing textbooks. But in the late evening, after her two sons were fed and safe in bed, Morrison began to finish the short story she wrote years ago when she lived in Washington, D.C. The short story she presented to the writers' group had become the plot for *The Bluest Eye.*

Morrison named the book's African-American narrator Claudia. Along with her sister Frieda, she is friends with Pecola. Like Pecola, Claudia and Frieda are poor, but their family life is more stable. Claudia's and Frieda's mother is strict, but nurturing. She demands that her daughters be well behaved, but Mrs. MacTeer takes good care of her children. When Claudia becomes sick with a bad cold, her mother insists that she stay in bed and rubs her neck and chest with a medicinal salve to help her get better.

On the other hand, Pauline, Pecola's mother, does not recognize that her daughter needs her love and support. After Pecola was raped, Pauline does not realize that Pecola is suffering. She beats Pecola at a time when Pecola desperately needs to be comforted. To escape her pain, Pecola hopes to become someone she is not—and she loses her mind when she comes to believe that her eyes have indeed changed, when in reality they have not.

To write *The Bluest Eye*, Morrison relied on her childhood memories of life in Lorain, Ohio. The young characters grow up in a neighborhood of people and places a lot like those Morrison knew as a child. But the similarity ends there. Morrison grew up with a strong sense of pride and love for her African-American heritage, while Pecola is rejected by her family and the other adults and children in her neighborhood. She has no positive role models for beauty and blackness.

For Pecola's mother Pauline, women like the film star Jean Harlow were very beautiful.

The story takes place in the early 1940s, and even Pecola's mother Pauline is drawn to white film stars, such as Jean Harlow, for her own standard of beauty.[1] Morrison's narrator Claudia tells Pecola's sad story years later as an adult when she comes to understand her friend's low self-esteem and her struggle against heartache and pain.

Morrison began writing *The Bluest Eye* in 1967, and continued to write during the eighteen months she worked in Syracuse. Morrison sent her almost completed manuscript to many publishers, but it was not quickly accepted by the industry. Morrison decided not to give the manuscript to Random House, since she felt it would be an awkward conflict of interest. However, an editor at another publishing company liked her work, offered her a contract, and encouraged her to finish the novel.

In late 1969, she received a job promotion at Random House and moved her family to New York City. Morrison was transferred from the textbook division to the trade division where she worked on books for the general readers' market. Morrison found a house in Queens and enrolled her two sons in a new school. The new senior editor position meant more exposure to the publishing field and more work, but Morrison tried her best to adjust. She continued to write at night to counter the loneliness and tremendous responsibility she felt as a single parent. Morrison discovered that writing gave her a sense of joy she had never known before. "Whether or not it [*The Bluest Eye*] was successful—or even whether or not it was published—I was committed already," Morrison said years later.[2] In an interview with *The Chicago Tribune*, Morrison told a reporter that the experience of writing her first novel was refreshing and brought a renewed sense of living.[3] The world outside her writing seemed far less interesting.

The Bluest Eye was published in 1970. Critical reviews of the novel were positive, though the sales were modest by publishing standards. Several reputable newspapers and book-review journals, such as *The New York Times Book Review*, *The Chicago Tribune*, *The New Yorker*, and *Newsweek*, reviewed *The Bluest Eye* and complimented Morrison for her writing style. Other reviews praised Morrison for daring to take an honest look at American racism and its damaging effects on the mental health and spiritual development of African-American children, particularly girls. Morrison was one of the first writers, black or white, to ask what happens to the mind, heart, and soul of a young African-American girl who is raised in a society that values beauty standards that are not her own.

"I've just finished reading Toni Morrison's

book, *The Bluest Eye*, and my heart hurts," wrote Ruby Dee, an African-American actress, in a review of the novel for a publication called *Freedomways*.[4] Dee wrote that she wanted to "lie down and cry" in response to the pain that young Pecola endures. Dee asked the reading public if, after reading *The Bluest Eye*, society can find a solution to one of the brutalities of racism—the reality of self-hatred. Dee encouraged both blacks and

Ruby Dee (shown here with her husband Ossie Davis) wrote a very positive review of The Bluest Eye.

whites to "think faster and work harder" to create a more humane society.[5]

The Bluest Eye did not bring immediate fame to Morrison, but she became a well-respected critic and spokesperson for African-American culture, life, and literature. Several scholarly journals and literary publications approached Morrison to write book reviews and essays on the need for social, political, and legal equality for women. A new crusade called the Women's Movement was beginning to capture the nation's attention in the early 1970s. While the Women's Movement worked to solve the problems of mostly white middle-class women who were raised to take care of their husband and family rather than pursue a profession, Morrison could speak to the problems of working-class black women, like her mother Ramah, and other members of her family. These women struggled against racism and low wages in an effort to support their families. As a result of her background, Morrison was eager to respond. As an African-American woman, she brought a unique perspective to many of the social, political, and literary debates of the time. Eventually, Morrison wrote more than twenty reviews, mostly for *The New York Times.*

The Civil Rights Movement made some legal strides with the passage of two major civil rights laws such as the Civil Rights Act of 1964, which forbids discrimination based on color, race, sex, religion, or national origin, and the Voting Rights Act of 1965, which forbids discrimination in voting. Despite these legal successes, blacks still did not enjoy many of the social, political, and economic rights that were given to whites. The door to racial equality was still not open, and the 1968 assassination of Dr. Martin Luther King Jr. left many African-Americans angry and disillusioned.

The point of view of black women in the literary and political circles of mainstream white society was invisible by the early 1970s. Two other African-American women, notably the poet Gwendolyn Brooks, winner of a Pulitzer Prize, and Lorraine Hansberry, the playwright, had been published in the 1960s, their writings were not generally used as material for literature courses in schools and colleges across the country. Nellie McKay, an editor and scholar of American and Afro-American literature, notes that at least fifty-nine books by African-American women were in print between 1859 (the publication year of *Our Nig* by Harriet Wilson, the first novel by a African-American woman) and 1964. And in the 1920s and 1930s, only one woman—Jesse Fauset—had published three novels.[6] While other African-American women writers had come before Morrison, few had received much notice for their work from mainstream literary circles. Morrison hoped to bring attention to African-American women writers and their role in literature.

Before the publication of *The Bluest Eye*, Morrison believed something important was missing from African-American literature—the voice of the African-American female. Morrison said African-American men wrote many of the novels she read. Writers such as James Baldwin, author of the novel *Go Tell It on the Mountain*, Richard Wright, author of *Native Son*, and Ralph Ellison, author of the novel *Invisible Man*, were well-received and read by blacks and whites. But "there were no books about me, I didn't exist in all the literature I had read . . . this person, this female, this black did not exist . . .," Morrison said in an interview with the *Women's Review* in London years later.[7] Although some women writers, such as Eudora Welty, Lillian Hellman, and Nadine Gordimer, present many different perspectives of white women in society, most contemporary white female authors did not examine the complex and rich life of black women. "Where is the white woman who has written what it feels like to hate the black women who reared her?" Morrison asked in the *Women's Review*. "I'd like to hear that."[8]

"There were no books about me, I didn't exist in all the literature I had read."

▲ 54 ▲

Morrison hoped that someday the number and impact of African-American women writers in American literature would change, but even after the publication of *The Bluest Eye* she did not think of herself as a real writer. She still thought of herself as a book editor and teacher. In 1971, she accepted another teaching position, this time at the State University of New York at Purchase. Morrison agreed to work as a visiting professor of English with a flexible schedule, teaching for only a year. Meanwhile, she continued her editorship at Random House.

Morrison did not publish her second novel until 1973. She spent nearly two and a half years writing the story of a very close friendship between two African-American women who live completely different lives and have different points of views about what makes life worth living. The idea for *Sula* did not come easily. Morrison spent quite some time imagining the plot for the story. During her morning rides on the subway from Queens to Manhattan, Morrison would think of characters and dialogue for her novel, anxious to get home at night to write her thoughts on paper. Before she began writing, Morrison knew she wanted to examine the dilemma between good and evil. "One can never really define good and evil," Morrison said years later in an interview with the *Massachusetts Review*. "It depends on what uses you put it to. Evil is as useful as good is."[9] In *Sula*, Morrison wanted to show that sometimes what society calls "evil" can also have a good purpose.

Morrison's characters, Sula and Nel, are the focus of the novel. Sula and Nel are born and raised in an African-American community called

Morrison after the publication of Sula

The Bottom, a tract of barren land given to a slave by a dishonest white landowner centuries earlier. The story takes place from 1919 to 1965. Sula and Nel are close friends as young girls and share most of their time and activities. As they grow older, their lives separate. Nel decides to remain in The Bottom after she gets married like most of the women in the town. Sula, however, leaves The Bottom to pursue an education and gain her independence from The Bottom's small-town ways. When Sula returns to the town ten years later, she has a series of affairs with several married men and even sleeps with Nel's husband, Jude. Soon, she becomes the outcast of the community. The men and women in The Bottom view Sula as an example of evil—a person with no conscience, a person who would do or say anything to satisfy her own desires. Sula is also criticized when she decides to place Eva, her grandmother, in a nursing home.

Despite her earlier friendship with Sula, Nel follows the popular opinion about her once-close confidante. She also views Sula as an outcast—until Sula's death. Nel is forced to come to terms with the truth of Sula's life and her own life choices. Nel must ask herself whether Sula was indeed "evil" or just misunderstood. Perhaps Sula was a good person who made bad choices—and those choices caused other people to view her as evil.

Sula dared to live her life outside the safe boundaries of her community, but she lived life on her own terms. Not many African-American women in the community had Sula's nerve or guts. Nel also wonders if the life she has led was indeed a good life, or a life lived in fear—the fear of rejection from her community or the fear of loneliness.

Literary editor and scholar Claudia Tate notes that Morrison did not consider herself to be a true writer until *Sula* was published.[10] Scholar and editor Karen Carmean agrees, pointing out that Morrison's second novel "challenges readers in ways *The Bluest Eye* does not, primarily because of Morrison's presentation of evil . . ." and the way her writing reveals that evil comes in many different forms.[11]

Critics had mixed reactions to the book. Some critics applauded Morrison for examining the reality of friendship between African-American women and for showing both the love and the estrangement that happen when two human beings relate to each other. Barbara Smith, a critic for *Freedomways*, wrote that Morrison was able to capture the strong bond between African-American women because she has personal knowledge of those relationships. "She has made a book for us that is beautiful, mysterious, and needed."[12] Scholar and editor Nellie McKay also credited Morrison for refusing to portray African-American women in a degrading way. In the past, few African-American women characters appeared in books. And the few that did exist were portrayed as menial workers or sexual objects. Instead, Morrison created a female character, Sula, who becomes a heroine while also being a social outcast.[13]

Other critics, however, chastised Morrison for writing about the darker side of human relations, rather than portraying characters in a more uplifting and positive light, or at least presenting some statement or opinion about characters, like Sula, who make unwise life choices. For example, one critic wrote that Morrison, and other writers with similar literary aims, ignore these moral dilemmas.[14]

Sula proved to be a critical literary success for Morrison, although the book's sales were not extravagant. The book was nominated for the 1975 National Book Award for fiction, *Redbook* magazine published portions of the book, and the *Nation* and the *Harvard Advocate* praised Morrison's work.

Morrison's reputation as a book editor was also highly respected. Her work at Random House made her an editor-mentor for other upcoming African-American writers whose first books she helped to publish. Authors such as Toni Cade Bambara, author of *Tales and Stories for Black*

Folks, Gayl Jones, author of *Corregidora*, and Henry Dumas, author of *Ark of Bones and Other Stories*, worked with Morrison. Morrison also edited biographies written by famous African-American figures, such as Andrew Young, the civil rights activist, Angela Davis, the political activist, and Muhammad Ali, the champion heavyweight boxer.

Morrison's next undertaking for Random House was an African-American historical scrapbook called *The Black Book*, published in 1974. Morrison worked with four collectors of African-American culture to create a scrapbook of photographs, newspaper articles, slave narratives, song lyrics, and other memorabilia dating back to the times of slavery and covering three hundred years of African-American history. The book was put together by Morrison and Middleton (Spike) Harrison; comedian Bill Cosby wrote the introduction. The research Morrison did for *The Black Book* would someday be the inspiration for one of her most famous novels.

In her personal life, Morrison continued to juggle her work schedule, her writing, and raising her two sons. She moved her family from Queens to Spring Valley, New York, and began a daily commute to and from Manhattan. To help manage her household finances, Morrison left the State University of New York at Purchase and accepted a visiting professor position at Yale University for the 1976–77 academic year. She agreed to teach a class on African-American women fiction writers while she also worked at Random House. To say the least, this left very little—if any—time for friends, or any social life at all. Morrison was still a single woman. "I considered marrying again, on several occasions, but I decided against it for two reasons," Morrison told *Time* magazine years later. "I didn't want to give up the delight of not having to answer to another person, and I was worried about how my two boys would react to a stepfather."[15] But the single life did not seem to bother her at all. "Sometimes I'll even forget to go if I've been invited to someone's house for dinner," Morrison would tell a reporter for *The New York Times* years later in an interview. "At this point in my life, anyone who's going to be a friend of mine is simply going to have to be able to understand that."[16]

However, the lack of male companionship in Morrison's life did not mean that she did not understand the male view of life, or that men did not interest her as characters for future novels. For example, Milkman Dead, the main character of Morrison's third novel, *Song of Solomon*, was born from Morrison's personal knowledge of the male mind and spirit. Morrison's father, George Wofford, died while she was writing the book, so

Morrison relied on her late-night conversations with his spirit to lead her through the manuscript. Morrison would imagine her father in her mind and communicate accordingly. In Morrison's family, a belief in the supernatural was a reality from which to draw strength and wisdom, and had never been something to fear. She learned this lesson as a child. Now, speaking to her father, Morrison found peace and guidance.

She relied on her experiences as the single parent of two sons and her relationship with her father to create Milkman. He was a man born in a small town in Michigan who leaves the Midwest to search for his family's roots in the South and learn whether or not it is possible to "fly."

Milkman Dead searches for peace of mind during his long journey to the South. His birth is quite an event—his mother Ruth gives birth to Milkman after she sees an insurance salesman, strapped in wings, try to fly off a hospital rooftop. The strange sight starts Ruth's labor and Milkman is born—the first black child born in a previously all-white hospital. Milkman's father, Macon Dead, the richest landowner in the African-American community, advises his son to follow in his footsteps by becoming a landowner, too. "The most important thing you'll ever need to know," Macon Dead declares, "[is to] own things. And let the things you own own other things. Then you'll own yourself and other people too."[17] Macon Dead is a man who believes that only money and property are the measure of a person's worth.

However, Milkman eventually defies his father's wishes and instead learns his family history from his aunt Pilate, a woman born with no navel, who carries a bag of bones, and wears a brass box for earrings. Milkman learns about a miner's sack of gold buried along a riverbank in the wilderness and leaves Michigan to search for it. Instead, he discovers his true family history and uncovers the legend of his great-grandfather Solomon and his "flight" from slavery to freedom in Africa.

Song of Solomon was published in 1977. It has become, perhaps, one of the best examples of why both literary critics and readers—black and white—in time have come to consider Morrison one of the finest novelists in America—and even the world. Critics note that in *Song of Solomon*, Morrison combined some of the most important elements of African-American culture, classic Greek literature, European-American literary styles, and Christianity. Critics noted that Morrison relied upon African-American and classical Greek folktales as the foundation for the plot. They said that she drew from myths of human flight—the legends of African slaves flying to freedom, and Daedalus, the ancient Greek who makes a pair of wings to escape prison with his son, Icarus. Morrison said later that her story was inspired by African folktales, not Greek mythology. Morrison also gave her characters common names from the Bible—Solomon, Pilate, Hagar, and Ruth. Scholar Karen Carmean notes that Morrison may have named her novel after her grandfather John Solomon Willis, in tribute to him.[18]

Morrison's ability to weave these elements into a complex and lyrical novel, with an African-American male character as its hero—a rare story plot for an African-American woman writer in the late 1970s—made *Song of Solomon* Morrison's most influential book. It won the National Book Critics Circle Award for fiction for that year and was also featured on the front page of *The New York Times Book Review*. Morrison was honored when *Song of Solomon* became a major book selection for the Book-of-the-Month Club, the only book written by an African-American to earn that tribute since Richard Wright's *Native Son* in 1940.

Critics no longer viewed Morrison as an aspiring writer. She had become an important literary presence in the publishing industry—a true writer. Melvin Dixon, a reviewer for a publication called *Callaloo*, called Morrison's novel a "brilliant, compelling achievement."[19] Samuel Allen, a critic for the *Boston University Journal*, wrote "the novel is the product of a skilled artisan," who managed to combine the two traditions of gospel and the classics.[20]

The U.S. academic and literary establishment agreed with the critics. In 1977, Morrison was appointed to the American Academy Institute of Arts and Letters, and President Jimmy Carter appointed her to the National Council on the Arts. However, even before Morrison received critical acclaim, she placed her faith in the book's eventual success and resigned from her position at Random House to devote herself to a full-time career as a writer and teacher. She left her visiting professorship at Yale University. Her belief in *Song of Solomon*'s success became a reality—the book was hailed as a triumph. Toni Morrison was now a well-recognized and respected American writer and intellectual. Her life would never be quite the same again.

CHAPTER FIVE

BELOVED

The tremendous success of *Song of Solomon* made it possible for Morrison to once again make important changes in her personal life. The book's sales enabled her to move from Spring Valley, New York, to a three-story, newly designed boathouse on the Hudson River in Grandview-on-Hudson, New York, in the early 1980s. She now worked only part-time at an editing position at Random House. She agreed to return to Random House to work on various editorial projects for the publisher, but her main concerns now were her writing and her private life.

Morrison took time out to tend a flower garden and she changed her writing hours from late at night to the early hours of the morning. She continued to write during quiet and peaceful times, but now she woke at 5:00 A.M, rather than falling asleep in the wee hours of the morning. Morrison would sit outside on her porch or on her own private dock on the river to jot down story ideas, characters, and dialogue. Morrison was already an intensely private person, and the increased solitude gave her even more time to write and read works by other authors.

While settling into her new home, Morrison began work on her fourth book, *Tar Baby*. The novel tells the story of a passionate, yet turbulent, love affair between a young, sophisticated, college-educated, and French-speaking black model named Jadine Childs, and Son Green, an African-American fugitive who escapes from Florida to an island called Isle des Chevaliers in the West Indies. It is on this island that Son meets Jadine and her uncle and aunt, Sydney and Ondine Childs, a butler and cook. The Childses work for Valerian Street, a wealthy white man who has retired from his candy factory in Philadelphia. Street and his wife Margaret move to the island and live in a mansion called L'Abre de la Croix. In Morrison's story Jadine and the Streets find Son in the mansion. Son is a thief who accidentally killed his wife. To escape the law, Son had gotten on a ship and jumped overboard, swimming to Isle des Chevaliers. Son's appearance causes an uproar in the home, but Valerian Street allows him to stay. During this short stay, Son and Jadine fall in love.

Jadine and Son, though from different economic and social backgrounds, have an affair.

Jadine runs off with Son to New York despite the fact that a rich man in France has asked her to marry him. In New York, Son realizes that he cannot adjust to Jadine's "superficial" world and her upper-middle-class values. He convinces Jadine to come with him to his hometown, Eloe, in Florida. However, Jadine is not satisfied with the simple, small-town country life of the South. The two lovers cannot come to terms with their differences, and Jadine's family in Isle des Chevaliers struggles to find peace when an old family secret of child abuse is discovered after Son is found in their home.

The clash of social and economic values between Jadine and Son is also part of their view of what it means to be black. Morrison based the plot of the novel partly on an African-American folktale called "Tar Baby." The folktale has its roots in West African culture. In Morrison's novel, some literary critics have come to interpret the folktale as symbolizing the differences in African-American social classes. There are many versions of the tale, but when Morrison wrote "Tar Baby" she used the version she heard as a child.

In this version, a white farmer makes a "tar baby" out of a mixture of tar and turpentine. He creates the figure to get rid of an annoying rabbit that has caused damage in his garden. The farmer dresses the tar baby in a skirt and hat and sets it in the garden to trap the rabbit. When Brer Rabbit sees the tar baby, he comes close and says "Good morning," hoping to hear a friendly reply. When the tar baby does not respond, the rabbit gets angry and hits the figure. Unfortunately, the rabbit gets stuck in the tar. When the farmer sees Brer Rabbit in the tar, the rabbit tries to fool the farmer with a rhyme. "Boil me in oil, skin me alive, but please do not throw me in that briar patch!" Not knowing the rhyme is a trick, the farmer throws the rabbit into the briar patch. The rabbit manages to escape, saying to the farmer, "This is where I was born and bred at!" The folktale was written by Joel Chandler Harris, a white American writer.

Critics view Morrison's use of the Tar Baby folktale in different ways. Critic Robert O'Meally, a reviewer for *Callaloo* magazine, wrote that Jadine represents the tar baby and Son represents Brer Rabbit. Son views Jadine as a kind of "tar baby"—a "tricky white man's creation set to waylay the black man." Son, meanwhile, is Brer Rabbit, whose home is down in the briar patch. At the end of the novel, O'Meally wrote that Son is "loosed from her grasp and runs: lickety-split, lickety-split."[1] Literature professor Karen Carmean writes that "Son and Jadine are opposites in the most essential ways, incompatible in their personal hopes and dreams. On the other hand, they can't entirely let go of each other, as if stuck to a tar baby."[2]

Although *Tar Baby* is the first Morrison novel to include white central characters—Valerian and Margaret Street—her use of the "Tar Baby" folktale shows her commitment to analyzing complex relationships between African-Americans and their cultural roots.

Tar Baby received mixed reviews when it was published in 1981. Some critics praised Morrison (who took three and a half years to write the book) for her lyrical language, her use of folktales, and the rich images she created to describe the people and places in the novel. However, other critics felt Morrison devoted too much energy to the book's imagery and not enough to the development of her characters or plot.

The book's reviews may have been mixed, but the media gave Morrison a lot of attention when the novel was published. *Newsweek* magazine featured Morrison on its front cover on March 30, 1981, to give readers an up-close and personal view of one of the country's finest writers. Morrison was the second African-American woman writer to receive such exposure—the first was Zora Neale Hurston, author of the 1937 novel *Their Eyes Were Watching God*. Hurston appeared on the magazine's cover some forty years earlier.[3]

"Are you really going to put a middle-aged, gray-haired colored lady on the cover of this mag-

Zora Neale Hurston was the first African-American woman writer to appear on the cover of Newsweek.

azine?" Morrison jokingly asked *Newsweek*'s editorial staff when she visited the publisher's office for the cover photograph.[4] The staff said "Yes," and they called the article, "Toni Morrison's Black Magic." The article appeared along with photos of

Morrison as a child, her parents, grandparents, and her two sons.

The *Newsweek* article gave many of Morrison's colleagues the opportunity to comment on her contributions to African-American and American literature. "Toni has done more to encourage and publish other black writers than anyone I know," said Andrew Young, the civil rights activist and politician.[5] Writer Toni Cade Bambara, a Morrison protégée, credited the author for her work as a "superb" editor and novelist. "The fact

James Baldwin praised Morrison's work in the Newsweek *article.*

that she is there, with her canny, spooky voice, gives other people inspiration to fly."[6] Perhaps one of the article's greatest compliments came from James Baldwin, the highly respected African-American writer. "We still overlook the incredible stamina—Toni would say 'sheer intelligence'—of black women in their ability to be all those things which somehow hold a black man together. Toni shows this, with a sense of humor, that is the key to a sense of life."[7]

Tar Baby sold extremely well on its own and made *The New York Times* best-seller list thirty days after its publication. Not long after *Tar Baby*'s release, Morrison told an interviewer she was pleased with her growth as a writer. She said that her goal was to become a better writer—not to become a success among critics or readers, who often commented that her novels were too complex. She believed her readers could meet the challenges presented by her work.

Two years after *Tar Baby*'s publication, Morrison finally decided to give up her part-time position at Random House. After completing her professorship at Yale University in 1977, Morrison served as a lecturer at Bard College in upstate New York in 1979. In 1984, she was appointed as the Albert Schweitzer Professor of Humanities at the State University of New York in Albany. Her new responsibilities included teaching creative writing and African-American literature, and helping students improve their skills in writing fiction. The new teaching position also made it possible for Morrison to try her hand at another artistic form—playwriting.

The New York State Writers Institute at the State University of New York at Albany, led by William Kennedy, a Pulitzer Prize-winning writer, contracted Morrison to write a play to honor Dr. Martin Luther King, Jr., and the observance of the first federal holiday celebrating the slain civil rights leader's birthday. The holiday is observed on the third Monday in January.

Once again, Morrison looked to African-American history and culture to create her play. She decided to base her work on the 1955 murder of a fourteen-year-old African-American boy named Emmett Till. The tragedy occurred one summer day when Till, a native of Chicago, visited family members in Mississippi. Till was shot twice in the head and beaten after a group of white men kidnapped him from his uncle's house. The men claimed Till had whistled at a young white woman named Carolyn Bryant a few days before at a local store, and they had come to punish him for the offense. Three days after the kidnapping, Till's body was found in the Tallahatchie River.

Till's death was a national horror. It motivated many African-Americans to work even harder for civil rights in the South. However, when the

*The story of the brutal murder of Emmett Till
inspired Morrison to write a play.*

men who killed Till went to trial, an all-white jury
found them not guilty of murder.

In Morrison's play, titled *Dreaming Emmett*,
Till overcomes death and returns to tell the audience—and the world—the truth about how he was
cruelly killed. In an interview with the press,

Morrison said the play was about "a boy's imagination," and the possibilities that exist if an African-American child's imagination is allowed to grow undisturbed by death. Said Morrison, "What is it like if his dreams are fulfilled?"[8] The play opened two weeks before the first observance of the King holiday in 1986.

The plot of Morrison's next novel, *Beloved*, also included details from a terrible period in African-American and American history—the time of slavery. While doing research several years earlier for *The Black Book*, Morrison found a newspaper article about a black woman named Margaret Garner who had escaped slavery in Kentucky and relocated to Ohio in an attempt to save herself and her children from the brutalities of her white slave master. The article told the story of how Garner had cut her baby daughter's throat with a jigsaw to prevent the slave catchers from finding her alive and bringing her back to the plantation in Kentucky. The article appeared in a newspaper called *American Baptist* in 1856.

Garner's story became the inspiration for the plot of *Beloved*, Morrison's fifth novel. The book would be the first in a three-part series of novels Morrison planned to examine the various kinds of love. In the novel, Morrison tells the story of a runaway slave named Sethe who escapes from her plantation, called Sweet Home, after arranging the escape of her children. Sethe hopes to meet her husband later at an agreed-upon destination. Pregnant with a daughter, Sethe manages to find her way to a small town outside Cincinnati, Ohio. She comes to the house of an African-American woman named Baby Suggs, her mother-in-law. When Sethe arrives, her baby daughter has been born, and her three other children are safe at Baby Suggs home. However, some time later, slave catchers from Sweet Home discover Sethe and her children. Rather than see her children

Morrison signs a copy of Beloved *for a fan.*

captured and enslaved, Sethe hits her two sons on the head with a shovel and cuts the throat of her infant daughter. A family member stops Sethe before she is able to harm her other daughter, Denver.

The novel begins in 1873, almost twenty years after the infant daughter's death. Sethe and Denver live alone together in Baby Suggs' home. Baby Suggs is dead. For several years, the home has been haunted by a ghost. The hauntings are so frightening that Sethe's two sons, who have recovered from their head injuries, run away—never to be found. Denver remains with her mother, who has become a social outcast in town because of the supernatural hauntings and the atrocity she has committed—killing her child. Paul D, a former slave who lived on the Sweet Home plantation with Sethe years ago, appears at Sethe's home and moves in with her and Denver. In time, Sethe and Paul D begin a romance, and the ghost begins to terrorize the family even more. In a fit of rage, Paul D manages to throw the ghost out of the home. But when they meet Beloved, a mysterious young woman who shows up at Sethe's home and tries to live with the family, the characters come to believe that the ghost has reappeared. In time, Sethe and Denver believe that Beloved is the ghost of the infant daughter who was killed years ago. Why has

Beloved come back? Why was she killed? Was her death necessary? Should Sethe be judged for her crime? The characters struggle with these questions throughout the novel, as well as coming to terms with the impact of slavery upon their lives.

Morrison hoped *Beloved* would tell not only Sethe's story, but the life stories of the millions of Africans who died, or survived, during slavery in the American South. To accomplish this task, Morrison buried herself in research and learned all she could about the Middle Passage—the journey of Africans who were transported from Africa to slavery in North and South America and the Caribbean. She also wanted to learn how the Africans were actually treated by their slave masters, but Morrison found few sources for her research. She did find some slave narratives—stories told by the slaves themselves—and the writings of slave owners. But even visits to museums revealed little information. She also relied on folktales and slave songs, but found little information about the horrors slaves faced. Morrison had hoped to learn about what she calls the "interior life" of slaves—their deepest and inner-most thoughts and feelings about the day-to-day struggle of their lives. However, few sources provided the story Morrison hoped to tell.

Morrison did not give up, however. She finally decided to leave the United States to do research in Brazil. In Brazil, she visited slave museums and found exhibits that included the actual chains and other iron fixtures used to punish slaves or to keep them from running away. These artifacts helped Morrison create a novel that came very close to the reality of life for African slaves—close to their interior lives. Morrison did not want to write about slavery as a social institution, or "slavery with a capital 'S.' It was about these anonymous people called slaves," she has said, and "What they do to keep on, how they make a life. What they are willing to risk, however long it lasts, in order to relate to one another."[9]

Morrison's dedication to her research paid off when *Beloved* was published in 1987. In the first seven days after its publication, the book made *The New York Times* best-seller list and received very favorable reviews from most critics. The scene of Sethe's infant daughter's death is riveting in the novel, *New York Times* reviewer Michiko Kakutani wrote, the murder is "so brutal and disturbing that it appears to warp time before and after into a single unwavering line of fate."[10] The *Los Angeles Times* called the novel a "masterwork" that should be kept "on the highest shelf in American literature."[11] Morrison dedicated *Beloved* to the 60 million Africans who some historians believed died during the Middle Passage to North and South America and the Caribbean.

The literary establishment was impressed with Morrison's work, but several other writers and critics became gravely concerned when *Beloved* did not earn the National Book Award or the National Book Critics Circle Award for the year, both very prestigious awards in publishing. After all, Morrison's earlier novels, for example, *Sula*, was nominated for the National Book Award in 1975, and *Song of Solomon* won the National Book Critics Circle Award two years later. Forty-eight African-American writers and critics wrote a letter to *The New York Times Book Review* to lament the fact that although Morrison's literary work was exceptional, she had not received national recognition for her efforts. The letter was published on January 24, 1988.

Three months later, Morrison's *Beloved* won the Pulitzer Prize for Fiction. The Pulitzer Prize is one of the most distinguished awards in America. Each year the award is given for excellence in journalism, literature, music, and drama. Joseph Pulitzer, a prominent newspaper publisher, established the award and it has been given to exceptional writers and artists since 1917.

Some literary critics raised their eyebrows after the prize was given to Morrison, noting that the letter in *The New York Times Book Review* may have influenced the Pulitzer Board's decision. The board, which selects the winners, made it clear that it was influenced only by the credibility of Morrison's work when it decided to give her the award. "Obviously the board was aware of the statement [letter], but, no, it didn't affect their decision," said Robert Christopher, secretary of the Pulitzer Board, when asked if the letter to *The New York Times* had an impact on the members. "I think there was some feeling that it would be unfortunate if anyone diluted the value of Toni Morrison's achievement by suggesting that her prize rested on anything but her merit."[12]

Morrison, who made it clear she was not aware of the letter before its publication, told *The New York Times Book Review* she felt the prize was given to her fairly, despite the "gossip and speculation" that surrounded the event. "In the end I feel as though I served the characters in the book well, and I hope the Pulitzer people are as proud of me as I am of them," Morrison said, calling the signed letter "a kind of blessing for me." Morrison believed her colleagues "appreciated the worth of my work for them." Said Morrison, "They redeemed me, but I am certain they played no significant role in the judgment."[13] Morrison later received the Pulitzer Prize at an award ceremony at Columbia University in New York.

Although Morrison had been given one of the

most important literary awards in the country, she did not neglect her teaching career. A month after *Beloved*'s publication, Morrison accepted an appointment to the Robert F. Goheen Professorship in the Humanities Council at Princeton University to teach creative writing. Morrison was very pleased with her position at the State University of New York at Albany, and she was not too anxious to leave the post. However, Princeton University's commitment to liberal arts and education convinced her that the new position was the right choice. "I take teaching as

"I take teaching as seriously as I do my writing."

seriously as I do my writing," Morrison said in an interview. "Princeton's notion of what constitutes serious teaching dovetails with mine. You get a small number of students who are working on projects and stay with them for a year or even two."[14] Morrison said her aim in teaching students is to "help writers best do what they do best."

The professorship, which began in 1989, allowed Morrison to teach courses in African-American studies, American studies, and women's studies. To accommodate her new teaching schedule, Morrison would eventually purchase another home in Princeton, New Jersey.

Morrison took five years to complete her next

Morrison gives a reading at Princeton University.

three projects, a sixth novel called *Jazz*, a book of literary criticism called *Playing in the Dark: Whiteness and the Literary Imagination*, and a book of political essays called *Race-ing Justice, EnGendering Power: Essays on Anita Hill, Clarence Thomas, and the Constitution of Social Reality.*

Morrison published the second novel in her three-part series on love in 1992. The book, *Jazz*, tells the sad tale of the undoing of Joe and Violet Trace, a married African-American couple who leave the segregated South to live in Harlem, New York City in the mid-1920s. Like other southern African-Americans, Joe and Violet hope to find work and a better way of life in the city. However, during the early 1920s, while African-American artists, writers, and musicians in Harlem thrive, African-Americans in the cities also face racial prejudice. During the summer of 1919, blacks in cities across the country, such as Chicago and Washington, D.C., barely survive the attacks of vicious white mobs. The violence was so bad that the riots became known as the "Red Summer."

In *Jazz*, Joe and Violet's marriage crumbles when Joe, a middle-aged man, falls in love with Dorcas, an eighteen-year-old woman. In a fit of passion, Joe shoots and kills his lover Dorcas. Violet, who finds out about the affair, later tries to cut the face of the young woman's corpse at the funeral. In this novel, Morrison examined the extremes of romantic love between a man and a woman.

Similar to some of her earlier works, Morrison relies on artifacts from African-American culture to create her story. The idea for the novel is taken from a book of photographs called *The*

Harlem Book of the Dead, by James Van Der Zee, a famous African-American photographer who worked during the Harlem Renaissance. A photograph of a young girl lying in a coffin—shot by her jealous ex-boyfriend—sparked Morrison's imagination for the story.

Once again, Morrison's work drew mixed reactions from critics. Some continued to praise Morrison for her lyrical writing style and gift of storytelling, while others felt the style was too cumbersome for readers to enjoy the plot. Literature professor Karen Carmean writes that Morrison selected the title *Jazz* because the word "originally was a slang term for sexual passion" and because the word is known "for the most famous kind of black music, a special kind of music that aspires to come from and produce pure emotion."[15]

Morrison tried to organize her novel like a piece of jazz music. Carmean writes that the novel, like jazz, has a "fast opening, establishing a dominant note and theme," and then the novel "breaks into different parts—various stories [passages] and voices [instruments] . . ."[16] Carmean writes that the novel is inspired "by the whole range of human feelings,"[17] just as jazz music is a musician's vision of human emotions and life experiences.

Morrison's book of literary criticism was quite

a departure from her focus on writing fiction. In *Playing in the Dark*, Morrison examined the role of race in the works of other famous fiction writers, notably Edgar Allen Poe, Mark Twain, Ernest Hemmingway, Willa Cather, and others, to understand their treatment of African-American characters. As a result of her studies, Morrison found that many white writers shortchanged American readers by simply avoiding black characters, or portraying them as stereotypes. However, when white authors dared to create black characters, Morrison wrote that literary critics did not attempt to point out how important the African-American characters were to American literature. She also found that literary critics were reluctant to comment on the racial point of view of white American authors. "Black people and black things and Africa-type things are understood to be blank space for white imagination," Morrison said in an interview with the *Washington Post*. "It's the 'Heart of Darkness.' No Africans talk in there."[18] *Playing in the Dark* was based in part on a series of lectures Morrison gave at Harvard University while she was writing *Jazz*.[19]

Race was also an important factor in *Race-ing Justice*, Morrison's collection of political essays. A year before the book's publication, the nation had focused its attention on the controversial confirmation hearings of Clarence Thomas, a conservative African-American judge and nominee for the U.S. Supreme Court. Anita Hill, an African-American law professor from Oklahoma, who worked with Thomas years earlier, accused Thomas of sexual harassment. The political debate between Thomas's denial of sexual harassment, and Hill's serious charges was fierce, particularly in the African-American community where no consensus could be found.

Morrison became concerned that important social and political issues were not being addressed in the furor over Thomas' confirmation, so she

Anita Hill accused Clarence Thomas of sexual harassment and sparked a national debate.

asked several scholars and intellectuals to write their opinion about whether Thomas or Hill had been given a fair hearing. Despite the allegations against him, Clarence Thomas was eventually approved for the Supreme Court by the U.S. Senate. *Race-ing Justice* was published soon after the political debate. Some critics praised the writers for their influential views on race and class, but commented that the essays seemed to be repetitive. The conservative press knocked the book for its liberal bent in favor of Hill and against Thomas.

While reviews for *Race-ing Justice* were lukewarm, *Jazz* and *Playing in the Dark* became bestsellers on *The New York Times* book list. However, the critical response to *Playing in the Dark* was not complimentary. Morrison's examination of racial stereotypes and attitudes in American literature did not win the approval of some political conservatives. Her findings were severely criticized in the conservative press, which insisted that Morrison had not contributed any worthy scholarship to the race debate.[20] However, many other scholars of African-American and American literature view *Playing in the Dark* as an important academic examination of American literature and culture.

Morrison took the criticism in stride. She was not disheartened. Instead, she devoted her time to another creative project that was also unveiled in

1992. Morrison had been contracted by Carnegie Hall a year earlier to write song lyrics to an original musical score written by composer André Previn. The project was called "Honey and Rue," a collection of songs that was eventually performed

Kathleen Battle sang the lyrics Morrison wrote for "Honey and Rue."

live and recorded by Kathleen Battle, the African-American opera singer.

Battle, in an interview for the project, said she thought Morrison would be a perfect match for the song collection when she thought of Morrison's novel *The Bluest Eye*. "I imagined as I read subsequent works of hers, how thrilling it would be to hear her words set to music," Battle said.[21] Morrison, in the same interview, was also excited about her creative contributions. "I was interested in the marriage of language and music," said Morrison. "The best of all possible things was to hear Kathleen sing the songs."[22]

Morrison's colleagues and critics would be surprised by the next achievement in her life. She was soon to be considered one of the finest fiction writers in the world.

CHAPTER SIX

WHAT IS PARADISE?

The Nobel Committee of the Swedish Academy in Stockholm, Sweden, made no one prouder than Toni Morrison was when it gave her the Nobel Prize in Literature in 1993. "I feel good about this, really good," Morrison said in an interview with the *Washington Post*. "Part of the pleasure is the fact that it was wholly unexpected. It's not a narrow, personal, subjective delight. I feel it on a very large scale."[1]

Morrison's family, friends, and colleagues rushed to congratulate her when they heard the news. Morrison was especially happy to hear from other African-American writers. "[The prize] feels expanded somehow, like a very large honor, because one can share it with more people than one's neighborhood, or one's family. I feel like it is shared among us [African-American writers]."[2]

The prize gave Morrison a sense of recognition she had not had before—even as the winner of a Pulitzer Prize. The Nobel's international scope could not be ignored, but Morrison, as usual, kept the honor and its prestige in perspective. "When I heard I'd won, you heard no 'Aw, shucks,' from me," Morrison told *Time* magazine. "The prize

Morrison said that she appreciated the award, but did not let it alter her view of herself.

didn't change my inner assessment of what I'm capable of doing, but I welcomed it as a public, representational affirmation of my work . . . I felt pride that a black and a woman had been recognized in such an international forum."[3]

Morrison returned from her weeklong celebration in Sweden in mid-December 1993, and went back to work at Princeton University where her colleagues and students shared in her happiness. Unfortunately, this joyous time ended when Morrison faced a personal tragedy just a few weeks after her return. Her Grandview-on-Hudson home in upstate New York burned to the ground on Christmas Day. Morrison's son, Slade, was home when the fire started, but fortunately no one was injured.

The fire was sudden and swift. It began at 9:00 A.M. after an ember from a fireplace landed on a sofa. According to press reports, Slade tried to put out the fire himself, but the flames burned out of control and he rushed to call the fire department. Soon after the fire trucks arrived, flames could be seen coming from the house's windows. Slade called his mother at Princeton University. By the time Morrison got there, her home was already demolished. Morrison made no comments to the press, but Howard Dodson, chief of the Schomburg Center for Research in Black Culture in New York, and a friend of Morrison's, told reporters that family members said she was "upset over the loss of the house." Immediately, both Morrison and Dodson were concerned about Morrison's original book manuscripts and whether they had been destroyed in the fire.

"The house was almost totally destroyed, but indications are that the major part of the manuscripts and other material in the basement were not severely damaged," Dodson told *The New York Times*.[4] However, since the fire, the surviving manuscripts have been kept at the Firestone Library in Princeton University. The manuscripts are being preserved and are not on view to the general public.

In a television interview three years after the tragedy, Morrison said that after the fire happened, she could not share her thoughts about it with anyone for quite some time. She became depressed and worried that she had lost belongings that could never be replaced, such as her children's report cards, or the original manuscript of her novel *Song of Solomon*. However, Morrison, later recovered, and decided to rebuild her home while she continues to live in Princeton, New Jersey, during the school year.

Morrison dedicated the next five years to writing the third novel in her three-part series on love. But in the meantime, she directed her energies to her responsibilities as a professor at

Princeton University. In 1994, Morrison created the Atelier (a French word meaning "artist's studio") Program at Princeton. The purpose of the program is to allow students to work together with professional artists and faculty members to create original projects in the visual arts, literature, music, dance, film, and theater. The students, artists, and faculty members meet in small groups at weekly workshops, in which the students work with the artists to develop a group project for the semester. The project can be an originally choreographed dance, an opera, a dramatic play, or a short film documentary, depending on what the group decides to work on. "There is a very complicated and exhilarating process that [the students] will go through when they work with people in other genres," Morrison said in an interview about the special program. "That's where the spark is."[5]

The program has received funding from the Samuel I. Newhouse Foundation, alumni, and friends of the university.[6] Students apply for admission to the program and are often recommended by faculty members. Morrison also participates in the workshops, giving her own creative guidance in addition to teaching her own creative writing classes.

Since the program began, several professional artists, including Bernice Johnson Reagon, founder of the a cappella gospel/folk group Sweet

Honey In The Rock, have participated in the Atelier. Jacques d'Amboise, a choreographer and lead dancer with the New York City Ballet, has also contributed, along with Yo-Yo Ma, a master cellist, A.S. Byatt, a master fiction writer, and Peter Sellars, a master director.

"We didn't feel like we were novices or were doing something that wasn't worthwhile," said Tom Ford, a classics major and 1997 Princeton graduate who participated in the program. Ford made his comments in an interview with *Princeton Alumni Weekly*. "The artists had the same sort of expectations of us that they would have had of people who were doing this professionally. They seemed to be operating under the same assumption that we were capable to doing something of genuine artistic worthiness and they were careful not to step on us creatively."[7]

In January 1995, Morrison and her family were honored by the Lorain Public Library in Morrison's hometown. The library opened the Toni Morrison Reading Room in Morrison's honor. Morrison was flattered and traveled back home to her family to attend a special opening ceremony. Several months later, in the spring, Morrison returned to her alma mater, Howard University in Washington, D.C., to receive a Doctor of Humane Letters degree—an honorary academic degree.

A year later, the National Endowment for the Humanities named Morrison the Jefferson

*Morrison cuts the ribbon on the Toni Morrison
Reading Room at the Lorain Public Library.*

Lecturer in Humanities for 1996. That honor is
the highest award given by the United States government for excellence and achievement in the
humanities. The award is given for "distinguished
intellectual achievement in the humanities." Morrison received a $10,000 cash award and delivered
a speech on modern humanity and the future at
the Kennedy Center in Washington, D.C. "Toni

Morrison is one of America's greatest contemporary novelists," said Sheldon Hackney, chairman of the National Endowment for the Humanities, which established the award in 1972. "Taking as her subject the cosmos of African-American experience and folklore, she brilliantly dramatizes in her novel the archetypal theme of the quest for individual and cultural identity and the sometimes confusing influence of family in that quest."[8]

In December 1996, Morrison was recognized by a new literary audience—the watchers of "The Oprah Winfrey Show." Oprah Winfrey, the popular African-American daytime talk show host, selected Morrison's novel, *Song of Solomon*, for the Oprah Winfrey Book Club. The result was a second wave of success for the novel. The book club, created by Winfrey, includes Winfrey's national audience of viewers. The viewers and Winfrey read the selected book and later a show is dedicated to the author and the book for an open discussion. Six audience members are chosen for a private dinner with Winfrey and the author to be broadcast at a later date.

Morrison had no idea of Winfrey's tremendous influence in the publishing industry and was not a regular viewer of "The Oprah Winfrey Show." "I'd never heard of such a thing," said Morrison when asked about the Oprah Winfrey Book

Club in an interview with *Time* magazine. ". . . All I could think was 'Who's going to buy a book because of Oprah?'"[9] According to Morrison, one million additional copies of *Song of Solomon* were sold, due to its selection for the book club, and sales of Morrison's other novels reportedly jumped 25 percent.

"All I could think was 'Who's going to buy a book because of Oprah?'"

Morrison's relationship with Oprah Winfrey would flourish creatively. Winfrey not only selected another Morrison novel, *The Bluest Eye,* for her book club, but she also purchased the movie rights to Morrison's novel *Beloved.* The movie became one of the most eagerly awaited films in recent years.

Morrison once again turned to writing song lyrics in 1997. This time, she collaborated with composer Richard Danielpour to write lyrics for original music called "Sweet Talk: Four Songs on Text." The project, which started in Morrison's Atelier program at Princeton University, debuted at Carnegie Hall in April 1997. Jessye Norman, the African-American opera singer, performed the songs in concert. "It's [writing lyrics] the only writing I do that is as close to thrilling as writing fiction," Morrison told a *USA Today* reporter.[10]

Morrison's third novel in her three-part series

Oprah Winfrey encouraged her viewers to read some of Morrison's books.

on love, *Paradise*, was considered long overdue by literary critics and readers. The novel, published in January 1998, was called Morrison's most ambitious book to date, and literary reviews were mixed. "I'm mad. Something I forgot to do is bothering me a lot," Morrison told *The New York Times* not long after the book's publication. "The last word in the book *Paradise* should have a small 'p,' not a capital P. The whole point is to get paradise off its pedestal as a place for anyone, to open it up for passengers and crew. I want all the readers to put a lowercase mark on that 'p.'"[11]

Paradise readers are taken to an all-African-American town called Ruby in Oklahoma in 1976. The town's history dates back to the 1870s when a group of African-American families, former slaves, leave the misery of Mississippi and Louisiana to search for freedom and prosperity in Oklahoma. Along the way, they meet other African-Americans at a town called Fairly, but they are rejected because of their dark skin tones. The men continue their travels and eventually start their own town called Haven. Haven becomes a close-knit rural community where everyone uses the same town oven to cook. No outsiders are allowed in the town. But after World War II, the close network of families and businesses begin to dwindle as people leave for the cities. The grandsons of Haven's founders pick up their families, take apart the town's oven, and move away to start a new town called Ruby. Like Haven, Ruby is also isolated and restricted from outsiders. It is located more than 90 miles (145 kilometers) from the nearest community, except for a small house of refuge for women called the Convent.

The novel begins when one of the women in the Convent—a white girl—is shot by a group of black male leaders from Ruby. The women's convent is considered to be a threat to the rigid morality in Ruby. The women, who have come to live together after surviving various life tragedies and misfortunes, practice a combination of an African and Christian religion. Some of the men in Ruby believe that the religion and the women are immoral, and so they decide to destroy the Convent and the women in it.

"The book coalesced around the idea of where paradise is, and who belongs in it," Morrison told a reporter for *The New York Times*. "All paradises are described as male enclaves, while the interloper is a woman, defenseless and threatening. When we get ourselves together and get powerful is when we are assaulted."[12] The race of characters is mentioned in other Morrison novels, however she does not reveal the race of the women at the Convent except for the first victim. "I did that on purpose," said Morrison in an interview with *Time* magazine. "I wanted the readers to wonder about the race of those girls until those readers understood that their race didn't matter. I want to dissuade people from reading literature in that way."[13]

In *Paradise*, Morrison also hoped to examine "the love of God and love for fellow human beings."[14] She wanted to explore why human beings, often influenced by religion, feel the need to create their own kind of "paradise" in society, and why creating a paradise often means other human beings must be excluded—as the men in Ruby exclude the women at the Convent.

Critics varied in their opinion of Morrison's work. Critic Louis Menand of *The New Yorker* said Morrison was "at the novelistic best."[15] Writer Paul Gray wrote in *Time* magazine that "Morrison's prose remains the marvel that it was in her earlier novels, a melange of high literary rhetoric and plain talk."[16] However, other critics complained that the book's plot was contrived. Michiko Kakutani wrote in *The New York Times* that *Paradise* is "a heavy-handed, schematic piece of writing."[17] Deirdre Donahue wrote in *USA Today* that the book is "hard to read and at times hard to understand," but that it is "worth the struggle."[18]

As usual, Morrison took the criticism in stride. She had hoped to work on the book's manuscript a bit longer, but there was no additional time before its publication date, which was moved up to the beginning of the year rather than spring. By March, Oprah Winfrey had selected *Paradise* for her TV book club and the novel had already made *The New York Times* best-seller list.

A few months later, Morrison's next creative venture appeared on movie screens across the country. The motion picture *Beloved*, based on Morrison's novel of the same name, opened in movie theaters in October 1998. Oprah Winfrey, who bought the movie rights to the film ten years earlier, co-produced the film and starred in the movie as Sethe, the runaway slave who kills her infant daughter and is later haunted by the infant's spirit. Many Hollywood insiders, and even

Morrison attends the premiere of Beloved *in New York City.*

Morrison herself, thought *Beloved* could not be made into a movie. The book was simply too complex and rich—the story of slavery too horrifying. But Winfrey persevered for ten years to select the right director and screenwriter for the project. Jonathan Demme, director of the Oscar-winning movie, *The Silence of the Lambs*, agreed to direct the movie. Richard LaGravenese, screenwriter for the movie *The Bridges of Madison County*, agreed to co-write the script.

Morrison, who visited the movie set while the film was being made, saw the completed movie three times before she could view it in an objective way. As the author of the book, Morrison knew it would be difficult not to see the movie through a writer's perspective. But she was finally pleased with the results. "They did something I thought they could never do: to make the film represent not the abstraction of slavery, but the individuals, the domestic qualities, and the consequences of it."[19]

Morrison also praised the cast of the film in a special appearance to promote the movie on "The Oprah Winfrey Show." Actor Danny Glover, known for his role in the "Lethal Weapon" movie series, played Paul D. Paul D not only appears at Sethe's home and becomes her love interest, but he also falls under the spell of the mysterious Beloved who has come to live with Sethe and Denver. Actress Thandie Newton, who appeared in the film *Jefferson in Paris*, portrays Beloved, and actress Kimberly Elise, who played in the movie *Set It Off*, portrays Denver. The star four-person cast impressed Morrison, who called the movie "extraordinary."

The critical reviews for the film were general-

Danny Glover and Oprah Winfrey in a scene from the movie Beloved

ly positive, although some were mixed and the movie's reception at the box office did not meet its high expectations. Critic Janet Maslin, in a review in *The New York Times*, praised director Jonathan Demme for "taking on the most enticing and daunting job of literary adaptation since *The English Patient*," and for succeeding "uncannily well in bringing the novel's pulse to the screen." Wrote Maslin, "*Beloved* works on its own, with only occasional confusing junctures. But it is much enhanced by the familiarity with the Pulitzer Prize-winning novel. In so ambitiously bringing this story to the screen, Ms. Winfrey underscores a favorite, invaluable credo: read the book."[20]

Critic Jack Matthews wrote in *New York Newsday* that Morrison's book is far better entertainment than the movie. "It [the story] works better as a novel than the movie. You can step back from the book, and in the case of *Beloved*, you must. Morrison weaves such a tight tapestry of history, romance, adventure, and metaphysical mystery that readers have to pause now and then to absorb and reflect. You can't do that with a movie."[21]

Audiences may have also been confused by the movie's complexity. However, movie insiders said *Beloved* failed to appeal to white moviegoers, resulting in poor sales at the box office. Although it took an $80-million investment to produce and market *Beloved*, it made only $8 million during its opening weekend in mid-October, and only pulled in $18 million by early November.[22] According to Ken Smikle of *Target Market News*, a research firm that tracks African-American media and consumers, the story of slavery is still a difficult tale to tell, unlike other historical tragedies such as the Holocaust. "You have to create empathy," Smikle told the *New York Daily News*, "and that's tricky."[23]

Despite Oprah Winfrey's immense popularity as a talk-show host, her own promotion of the film, and the quality of the acting and film direction, *Beloved*'s commercial success was marginal by film-industry standards. However, neither Winfrey nor Morrison plan to give up making movies. Winfrey has also purchased the movie rights to *Paradise* and may produce another motion picture for the big screen.

Morrison has achieved a great deal since her working-class beginnings in Lorain, Ohio, and lone writing sessions in Syracuse, New York. She is one of the finest fiction writers—of any race—in the United States and the world. She is a popular guest speaker and receives hundreds of requests to speak at colleges, universities, and bookstores around the country. She is also a successful parent—her sons, Ford and Slade, are now grown men. Ford is an architect and Slade, the father of a daughter named Kali, is a painter.

Today, Morrison helps to fight oppression

Morrison after a speaking engagement in New York

against people of color all over the world. She is a
member of the Universal Academy of Cultures in
Paris, France. Along with other Nobel Prize winners, artists, and scholars, she is working to write
an international manual against racism. In her

role as a teacher and academic, she is helping to shape the lives of the next generation of writers and artists who also believe creativity can be used to lift the human spirit and to tell the story of those whom society often forgets. Morrison has become an important literary voice for African-Americans, women, and all others who have been excluded from America's "paradise."

Literature scholars and students who respect and admire Morrison's work come together every two years in a conference to present research papers about her novels. The conferences are sponsored by the Toni Morrison Society and began in 1998. The scholars have presented papers on topics such as the meaning of home and the portrayal of the South in Morrison's writing.

The Society's most recent conference was held September 28-October 1, 2000 at Lorain Community College in Elyria, Ohio, not far from Lorain where Morrison was born. As a matter of fact, the Society holds its conferences in or near cities that have meaning in Morrison's life. The Society's first conference, for example, was held in Atlanta, Georgia, a half-hour drive from Cartersville, where Morrison's father was born. Morrison attended the first conference and gave a special reading of her work.

The conference at Lorain Community College included a panel discussion on Morrison's work featuring Cornel West, the African-American scholar and theologian, Bell Hooks, John Edgar Wideman, and Marita Golden, all African-American authors. A seminar on how to teach Morrison's novels in high school English classes was held, as well as a tour of Lorain.

The Toni Morrison Society was created in May 1993, by Dr. Carolyn Denard, a professor at Georgia State University in Atlanta, during a meeting of the American Literature Association. The purpose of the Society is to "initiate, sponsor, and encourage critical dialogue, scholarly publications, conferences, and projects devoted to the study of the life and works of Toni Morrison."

"My responsibilities are to do the best work I can do and to be the best human being I can be," said Morrison in an interview with *Essence* magazine in 1998. "What [the Nobel] does—which is one of my assumed responsibilities—is to make it thinkable, possible, doable, for others. Other African-Americans and other women. If one, then why not two? If two, why not twenty? If I'm able to keep learning, putting myself in a position to learn something else, and putting myself in positions where

> "My responsibilities are to do the best work I can do and to be the best human being I can be,"

I can make it possible for somebody else to learn something, those are the major successes."[24]

Toni Morrison is more than a success. She is an inspiration for all writers, artists, and book readers. She is, as she likes to think of herself, a writer. A great American writer.

END NOTES

CHAPTER ONE

1. "Toni Morrison is '93 Winner of Nobel Prize in Literature," by William Grimes, *The New York Times*, October 8, 1993.
2. Ibid.
3. "Morrison's Slice of Paradise," by Deirdre Donahue, *USA Today*, January, 1998.
4. Ibid #1.
5. Ibid #1.
6. "Paradise Found," by Paul Gray, *Time* magazine, January 19, 1998.
7. "Nobel Lecture 1993," by Toni Morrison, *World Literature Today*, Winter, 1994.
8. "Author Toni Morrision Wins Nobel Prize," by David Streitfeld, *Washington Post*, October 8, 1993.
9. Ibid.
10. "Toni Morrison: Solo Flight Through Literature into History," by Trudier Harris, *World Literature Today*, Winter, 1994.
11. "Paradise Found," by Paul Gray, *Time* magazine, January 19, 1998.

CHAPTER TWO

1. "Nobel in Literature Goes to Toni Morrison," by Amy Gameron, *Wall Street Journal*, October 8, 1993.
2. "The Laureate's Life Song," by David Streitfeld, *Washington Post*, October 8, 1993.
3. *Critical Essays on Toni Morrison*, edited by Nellie Y. McKay, G.K. Hall & Co., 1988, page 49.
4. Ibid, page 52.
5. *Toni Morrison: Author*, by Douglas Century, Chelsea House Publishers, 1994, page 24.
6. "60 Minutes" transcript, March 8, 1998.
7. Ibid #5, page 23.
8. Ibid #6.
9. *Toni Morrison: Nobel Prize-Winning Author*, by Barbara Kramer, Enslow Publishers, 1996, page 18.

CHAPTER THREE

1. *Toni Morrison: Author*, by Douglas Century, Chelsea House Publishers, 1994, page 35.
2. *Toni Morrison: Nobel Prize-Winning Author*, by Barbara Kramer, Enslow Publishers, 1996, page 26-27.
3. Ibid, page 29.
4. Ibid, page 28.
5. *Critical Essays on Toni Morrison*, edited by Nellie Y. McKay, G.K. Hall & Co., 1988, page 43.

CHAPTER FOUR

1. *Toni Morrison's World of Fiction*, by Karen Carmean, The Whitson Publishing Co., 1993 page 21.
2. *Toni Morrison: Author*, by Douglas Century, Chelsea House Publishers, 1994, page 43.

3. Ibid, page 43.
4. *Critical Essays on Toni Morrison*, edited by Nellie Y. McKay, G.K. Hall & Co., 1988 page 19.
5. Ibid, page 20.
6. Ibid , page 2.
7. Ibid, page 45.
8. Ibid, page 46.
9. Ibid #1, page 44.
10. Ibid #1, page 31.
11. Ibid, page 31.
12. Ibid #4, page 24.
13. Ibid, page 4.
14. *Toni Morrison: Nobel Prize-Winning Author*, by Barbara Kramer, Enslow Publishing, 1996, pages 44–45.
15. "Paradise Found," by Paul Gray, *Time* magazine, January 19, 1998
16. Ibid #14, page 42.
17. Ibid #4, page 27.
18. Ibid #1, page 46.
19. Ibid #4, page 29.
20. Ibid, page 32.

CHAPTER FIVE

1. *Critical Essays on Toni Morrison*, edited by Nellie Y. McKay, G.K. Hall & Co., 1988, page 35.
2. *Toni Morrison's World of Fiction*, by Karen Carmean, The Whitson Publishing Company, 1993, page 64.
3. *Toni Morrison: Nobel Prize-Winning Author*, by Barbara Kramer, Enslow Publishing, 1996, page 56.
4. "Toni Morrison Magic," by Jean Strouse, *Newsweek*, March 30, 1981.
5. Ibid.
6. Ibid.
7. Ibid.
8. *Toni Morrison: Author*, by Douglas Century, Chelsea House, 1994, page 73.

9. *Toni Morrison's World of Fiction*, by Karen Carmean, The Whitson Publishing Co, 1993, page 83.
10. "Toni Morrison's Novel 'Beloved' Wins The Pultizer Prize in Fiction," by Dennis Hevesi, April 1, 1988.
11. Ibid #8, page 78.
12. Ibid #10.
13. Ibid#10.
14. "Creating The Danger I Need," by Angela Delli Santi, *Time Off*, December 2, 1987.
15. *Toni Morrison's World of Fiction*, by Karen Carmean, The Whiston Publishing Company, 1993, page 102.
16. Ibid.
17. Ibid.
18. "The Laureate's Life Song," by David Streitfeld, *Washington Post*, October 8, 1993.
19. Ibid #8, page 90.
20. Ibid #8, page 90.
21. "Honey and Rue," CD performed by Kathleen Battle, Liner Notes, page 3, Deutsche Grammophon.
22. Ibid.

CHAPTER SIX

1. "Author Toni Morrison Wins Nobel Prize," by David Streitfeld, *Washington Post*, October 8, 1993.
2. Ibid.
3. "Paradise Found," by Paul Gray, *Time* magazine, January 19, 1998.
4. "Toni Morrison's Manuscripts Spared in Christmas Fire," by Robert McFadden, *New York Times*, December 28, 1993.
5. "Morrison Organizes Program to Feature Writing, Theatre," by Howard Gertler, *The Daily Princetonian*, November 8, 1993.
6. "Toni Morrison's Atelier," by Deborah A. Kaple, *Princeton Alumni Weekly*, September 10, 1997.
7. Ibid.

8. "Morrison Wins Appointment as 1996 Jefferson Lecturer," by Mandy Terce, *The Daily Princetonian*, February 5, 1996.
9. Ibid #3.
10. "Morrison's Slice of Paradise," by Deirdre Donahue, *USA Today*, January, 1998.
11. "Toni Morrison's Mix of Tragedy, Domesticity, and Folklore," by Dinitia Smith, *The New York Times*, January 8, 1998.
12. Ibid.
13. Ibid #3.
14. Ibid #10.
15. Ibid #11.
16. Ibid #3.
17. Ibid #11.
18. "Morrison's Painful, Profound Paradise," Deirdre Donahue, *USA Today*, January 8, 1998.
19. "The Beloved Oprah," by Richard Corliss, *Time* magazine, October 5, 1998.
20. "No Peace From a Brutal Legacy," by Janet Maslin, *The New York Times*, October 16, 1998.
21. "A Restless Spirit Haunts Beloved," by Jack Matthews, *Newsday*, October 16, 1998.
22. "Cry, The Beloved Letdown," by Lewis Beale, *New York Daily News*, November 23, 1998.
23. Ibid.
24. "Paradise Found," *Essence* magazine, February, 1998.

CHRONOLOGY

1931　Born Chloe Anthony Wofford in Lorain, Ohio, on February 18.

1949　Graduates from Lorain High School.

1953　Graduates from Howard University with a bachelor's degree in English; enters Cornell University in Ithaca, New York.

1955　Receives masters degree in English from Cornell University; teaches English at Texas Southern University in Houston, Texas.

1957　Teaches English at Howard University in Washington, D.C.

1958　Marries Harold Morrison.

1961　Gives birth to son Harold Ford.

1962　Joins writers' group at Howard University.

1964　Resigns from teaching at Howard University; divorces Harold Morrison; moves to Ohio; gives birth to second son, Slade Kevin.

1965　Accepts job working as an editor for Random House in Syracuse, New York; moves to New York from Ohio.

1969　Receives promotion and becomes senior editor; moves to New York City.

1970　Publishes *The Bluest Eye.*

1971   Teaches English at the State University of New York at Purchase.

1973   Publishes *Sula*.

1974   Publishes first reference book, *The Black Book*.

1976   Teaches English at Yale University in New Haven, Connecticut.

1977   Publishes *Song of Solomon*.

1979   Serves as a lecturer at Bard College in Annadale-on-Hudson, New York.

1981   Buys a new home in Grandview-on-Hudson, New York. Publishes *Tar Baby*.

1984   Teaches creative writing at the State University of New York at Albany.

1986   Her play, *Dreaming Emmett*, is produced in New York.

1987   Publishes *Beloved*.

1988   Wins the Pulitzer Prize for fiction for *Beloved*.

1989   Accepts the Robert F. Goheen chair at Princeton University in Princeton, New Jersey; teaches creative writing and humanities courses at Princeton.

1992   Publishes *Jazz*; edits collection of essays on the Anita Hill–Clarence Thomas hearings called *Racing Justice, En-Gendering Power*; contributes song lyrics to "Honey and Rue," an original music score.

1993   Wins the Nobel Prize in literature for her novels; her home in Grandview-on-Hudson is destroyed by fire.

1994   Creates Atelier Program at Princeton University.

1995   The Toni Morrison Reading Room is opened at the Lorain Public Library in Lorain, Ohio.

1996   National Endowment for the Humanities names Morrison the Jefferson Lecturer in Humanities; *Song of Solomon* is selected for the Oprah Winfrey Book Club.

1997   Contributes song lyrics to "Sweet Talk: Four Songs in Text," an original music score.

1998   Publishes *Paradise*; *Beloved*, the movie based on Morrison's novel, is released.

A NOTE ON SOURCES

My first step in researching was to contact Alfred A. Knopf, the New York book publishing company that published Toni Morrison's most recent novel, *Paradise*, in 1998. I wrote the company a letter to ask if I could interview Morrison and get more information about Morrison and her life. While the company said no to an interview, they did send me a packet with copies of articles on Morrison.

Next I visited my local library to learn more about Morrison's life and the importance of her writing to American literature. I found several books that helped me, including *Toni Morrison: Author* by Douglas Century, *Toni Morrison: Nobel Prize-Winning Author* by Barbara Kramer, *Critical Essays on Toni Morrison*, edited by Nellie Y. McKay, and *Toni Morrison's World of Fiction* by Karen Carmean.

Besides books, I also found more newspaper and magazine articles and I ordered transcripts and video tapes from shows that Morrison had appeared on, including "60 Minutes" and "The Oprah Winfrey Show."

FOR MORE INFORMATION

BOOKS BY TONI MORRISON

Beloved. Alfred A. Knopf, 1998.
The Big Box. Hyperion Press, 1999.
The Bluest Eye. Alfred A. Knopf, 2000.
Jazz. Alfred A. Knopf, 1992.
Paradise. Alfred A. Knopf, 1997.
Song of Solomon. Plume, 1987.
Sula. Alfred A. Knopf, 1973.
Tar Baby. Alfred A. Knopf, 1987.

BOOKS ABOUT TONI MORRISON

Bloom, Harold, ed. *Toni Morrison*. Chelsea House Publishers, 1999.
Century, Douglas. *Toni Morrison: Author*. Chelsea House Publishers, 1994.
Kramer, Barbara. *Toni Morrison: Nobel Prize-Winning Author*. Enslow Publishers, 1996.
Patrick-Wexler, Diane. *Toni Morrison*. Raintree/Steck-Vaughn, 1997.

MAGAZINE ARTICLES ABOUT TONI MORRISON

"The Beloved Oprah," by Richard Corliss, *Time* magazine, October 5, 1998.

"Creating the Danger I Need," by Angela Delli Santi, *Time Off,* December 2, 1987.

"Paradise Found," *Essence Magazine*, February, 1998.

"Paradise Found," by Paul Gray, *Time* magazine, January 19, 1998.

"Toni Morrison's Magic," by Jean Strouse, *Newsweek*, March 30, 1981.

ORGANIZATIONS AND ONLINE SITES

The African-American Mosaic Exhibition
http://www.loc.gov/exhibits/african/intro.html
Discover some of the history that inspired Morrison's work from this online resource guide from the Library of Congress.

Africana.com
http://www.africana.com/tt_196.htm
Read a biography of Toni Morrison and explore the lives of other famous African-Americans.

Nobel Prize Internet Archive
http://nobelprizes.com/nobel/literature/1993a.html
Lists books by and about Morrison, her Nobel acceptance speech, a biography, interviews with Morrison, a bibliography, and excerpts from *Beloved.*

Time Magazine
http://www.time.com/time/magazine/1998/dom/980119/cover1.html

Read the cover story on Toni Morrison from the January 18, 1998 issue of *Time* magazine.

The Toni Morrison Society
http://www.gsu.edu/~wwwtms.index.html.
The Toni Morrison Society publishes a newsletter twice a year and maintains a website through the English Department at Georgia State University.

INDEX

ABOUT THE AUTHOR

Lisa R. Rhodes is a journalist and author of children's literature. She is the author of *Barbara Jordan: Voice of Democracy*, and a graduate of Baruch College, City University of New York, and the Columbia Graduate School of Journalism.